The Work of His Fingers

Alison Brown

THE BANNER OF TRUTH TRUST

THE BANNER OF TRUTH TRUST
3 Murrayfield Road, Edinburgh EH12 6EL, UK
P.O. Box 621, Carlisle, PA 17013, USA

*

© Alison Brown 2007

*

ISBN-13: 978 0 85151 965 4

*

Typeset in Myriad Pro at
The Banner of Truth Trust,
Edinburgh

Printed in the USA by
Graphics TwoFortyFour Inc.

Dedicated with love
to my husband David,
who shares my delight in
the study of the book of Genesis.

When we pause to consider this wonderful earth,
we see some incredible sights…

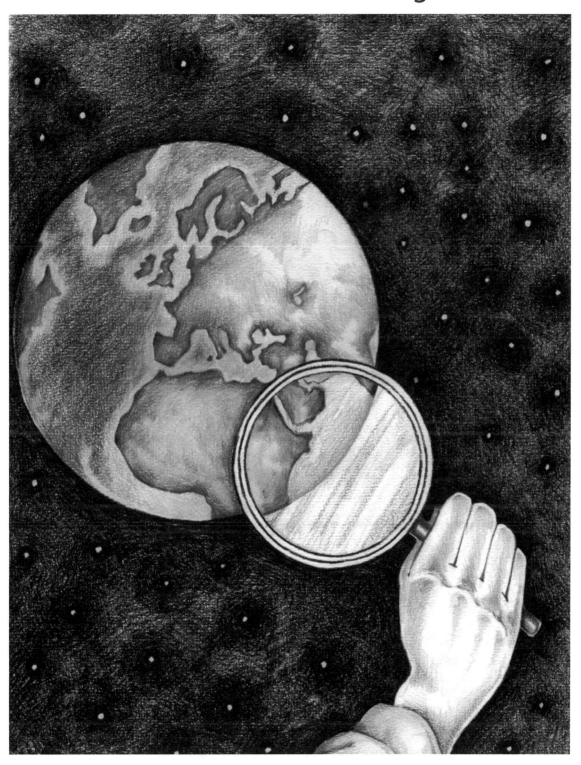

a world full of beauty suspended in space,
with billions of twinkling lights!

Perhaps you have wondered just how it got there,
… perhaps you've been tempted to guess?
(It didn't explode from a cloud of hot gas;
explosions make only a mess!)

Instead it was lovingly made by our God,
whose power and great understanding
are far beyond anything thought of by man;
no problem was found too demanding.

What distance to set from the earth to the sun
was a very important decision,

for only God knew what that distance should be,
and he measured with careful precision.

If too near the sun then our ground would burn up,
the grass would just wither and twist;
yet if too far away . . . all our water would freeze
and life could no longer exist!

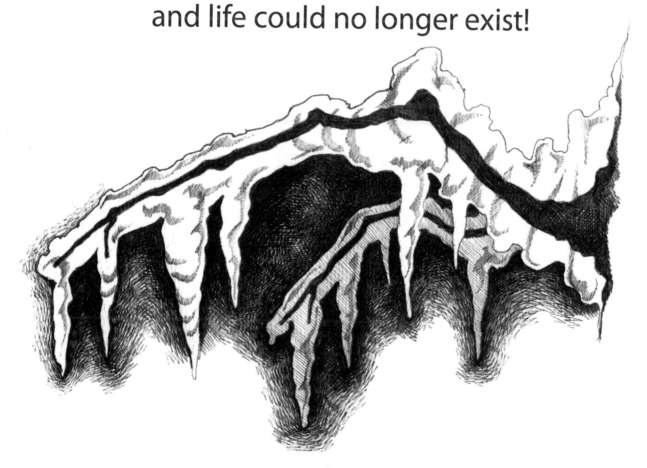

But God knew exactly just how to create
an atmosphere perfect for plants . . .

and since it's still here after thousands of years,
it could never have happened by chance!

Sometimes children ask us, 'How long is a year?
And how will we know when it's done?'

God ordered our years by the time that it takes
the earth to go once round the sun.

Our planet spins round as it travels along,
(each spin makes a night and a day);

the side next the sun will be flooded with light

while the other is gloomy and grey.

For people grow tired and their bodies must rest,
so God planned our time with dark spaces,
when shadows would fall and we'd want to lie
down . . .

in cosy and comfortable places.

As well as the sun, our great energy source,
God knew we'd need plenty of air;
he didn't put any on Venus or Mars
. . . no men would be living out there.

(If you go exploring in those barren worlds
you'll have to make up for the lack,
by breathing some oxygen out of a tank
you'll carry around on your back!)

And oxygen also protects us from harm
by forming a dense ozone layer

to soak up the deadly invisible rays
that come from the sun's dazzling glare.

This blanket of ozone is wrapped round the earth
ten miles or so up in the sky;

if God hadn't thought about putting it there
then everything living would die!

And then there is water . . . we always need some
for bathing or having a drink,
and doing the jobs that we may not enjoy
like washing those things in the sink!

But no other planet has water like ours,
collected in oceans and seas . . .
with vapour . . . and storm clouds . . .
and rain pouring down,
and taps running just where we please!

God created a world where
seasons can change . . .

new blessings
are sent from above;

through summer and autumn
and winter and spring

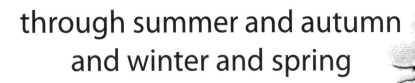

he dresses the earth
with his love!

We have flowers and bees and fruit-laden trees
in breathtaking colours and shapes . . .

with things we can look at, and things we can eat,
like pineapples . . .

peaches . . .

and grapes!

Take a look inside these and you'll be amazed,
by patterns of structure and line;
they had to be planned by someone who thinks . . .
such order appears by design!

Every plant carries seed, a true germ of itself,
which will root and grow into another . . .

so plums will grow plums . . .

and peas will grow peas . . .

baby plants all resemble their mother!

And animals too, as the Bible explains,
will produce only 'after their kind'.

'Like gives rise to like', as the scientists say,
(that's exactly what God had in mind.)

Giraffes will give birth to . . .

baby giraffes . . .

a chick is produced by a hen.

A frog will have spawn . . .

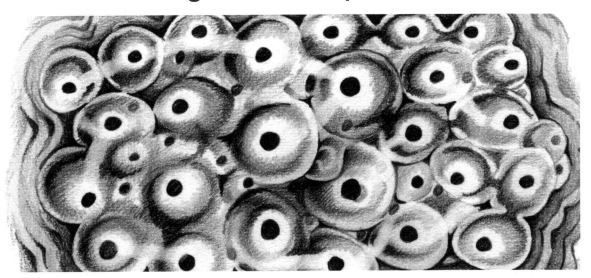

and tadpoles . . .

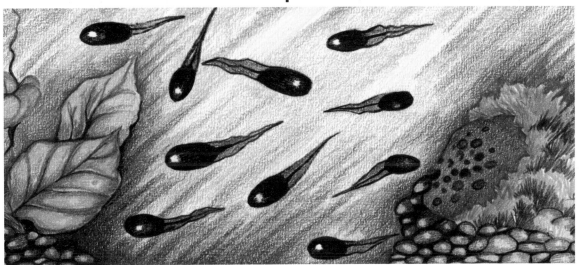

and frogs . . .

... but monkeys will never make men!

For we have been made in the image of God
with longings to know him as friend.
He gave us a mind that could study his Word . . .

and a soul that would live without end.

And let's not forget the great rule of science
that, 'Life can come only from life.'
The Creator *must live* who gave the first breath,
to Adam, and then Eve his wife!

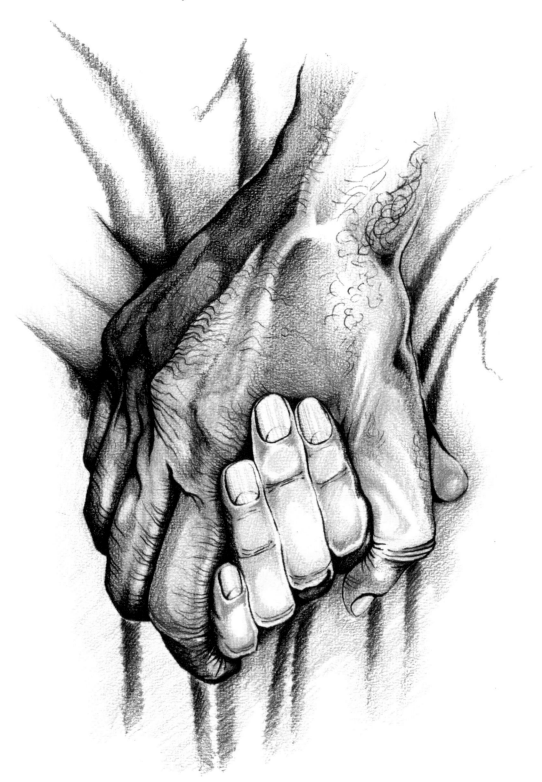

There's no need to debate or question or doubt
what God has so wonderfully done . . .

for the evidence all around us agrees
with Genesis chapter one!